Cliff Dwellers

By Linda Cernak

Scott Foresman
is an imprint of

Glenview, Illinois • Boston, Massachusetts • Chandler, Arizona •
Hoboken, New Jersey

Photographs

Every effort has been made to secure permission and provide appropriate credit for photographic material. The publisher deeply regrets any omission and pledges to correct errors called to its attention in subsequent editions.

Unless otherwise acknowledged, all photographs are the property of Pearson Education, Inc.

Photo locators denoted as follows: Top (T), Center (C), Bottom (B), Left (L), Right (R), Background (Bkgd)

Opener: ©Rod Pilcher/Alamy; **1** ©Ivor Kerslake/©DK Images; **3** ©Nathan Benn/Alamy Images; **4** (BR) cretolamna/Fotolia, (TL) Maimento/Fotolia, Meliha Gojak/Fotolia, (TR) villorejo/Fotolia, simmittorok/Fotolia; **5** ©Picture Contact/Alamy Images; **6** (Bkgd) ©Stefano Amantini/Atlantide Phototravel/Corbis, (Inset) ©Tony Souter/©DK Images; **7** ©Andy Holligan/©DK Images; **8** ©Rod Pilcher/Alamy; **9** ©Jason O. Watson/Alamy Images; **10** ©Alexey Stiop/Alamy; **11** ©Rod Pilcher/Alamy Images; **12** (BR) ©Chuck Place/Alamy Images, (BL) ©George H. H. Huey/Corbis, (T) ©North Wind Picture Archives/Alamy Images; **13** (BR) ©Jules Frazier/Getty Images, (T) ©Gianni Dagli Orti/The Art Archive at Art Resource, NY, (BL) ©Rob Shone/©DK Images; **14** ©George H.H. Huey/Alamy Images; **15** ©Stefano Amantini/Atlantide Phototravel/Corbis; **16** ©worker/Fotolia.

ISBN 13: 978-0-328-47279-6
ISBN 10:   0-328-47279-4

Copyright © by Pearson Education, Inc., or its affiliates. All rights reserved. Printed in Mexico. This publication is protected by copyright, and permission should be obtained from the publisher prior to any prohibited reproduction, storage in a retrieval system, or transmission in any form or by any means, electronic, mechanical, photocopying, recording, or likewise. For information regarding permissions, write to Pearson Curriculum Rights & Permissions, 221 River Street, Hoboken, New Jersey 07030.

Pearson® is a trademark, in the U.S. and/or in other countries, of Pearson plc or its affiliates.
Scott Foresman® is a trademark, in the U.S. and/or in other countries, of Pearson Education, Inc., or its affiliates.

How Do We Find Out About the Past?

Did you know that you can find clues about the past under layers of soil? People who search for clues about the past are called archaeologists. They look for artifacts, objects made and used by people who lived long ago.

Archaeologists look for artifacts.

Artifacts can tell us about how people once lived. An artifact might be a tool or a broken pot. Objects such as animal bones and plant remains can show us what people once ate.

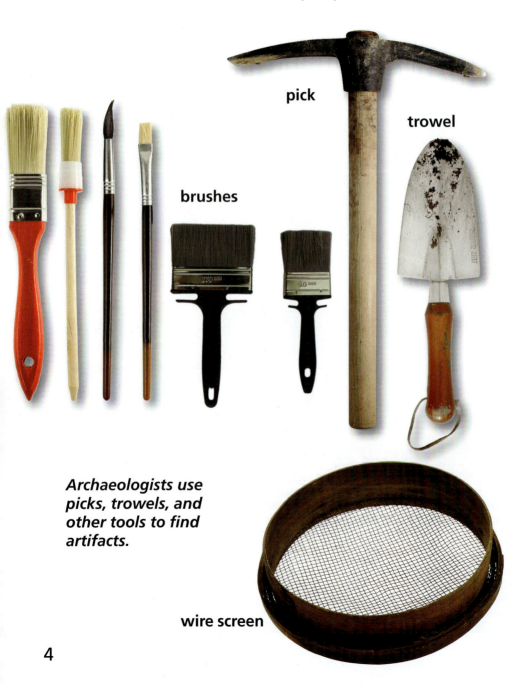

Archaeologists use picks, trowels, and other tools to find artifacts.

A piece of clay pottery might suggest how people once cooked. A part of a wall might show what kind of shelter a person lived in. A stone tool might show how people hunted. These clues give a picture of how people lived long ago.

Archaeologists study and ask questions about the artifacts they find.

Who Lived Here Long Ago?

More than 1400 years ago, people we call the Anasazi began to build homes in what is now part of Colorado. Today, archaeologists dig at these sites. They have learned much about the Anasazi and the pueblos they lived in.

Mesa Verde area of the southwest United States

Early cliff dweller's drawing

Pueblo comes from a Spanish word that means "town" or "village." It also refers to the different groups of American Indians who once lived in the Southwest. Some Pueblo people still live there.

Archaeologists have found thousands of artifacts in Mesa Verde National Park.

Many Anasazi lived in cliff dwellings. The dwellings were cut out of and built on canyon walls. These dwellings had one or more stories, similar to our modern apartment buildings.

This cliff dwelling, called Cliff Palace, has more than 150 rooms.

The cliff dwellings were built with stone tools. The Anasazi cut stones for the dwellings with sharp axes. They mixed mud and water to make mortar. The mortar held the stones of the buildings together.

The Anasazi built their homes with stones and mortar.

Round rooms called kivas were often built inside the cliff dwellings. Families used the kivas for social events and sometimes as a place to sleep. They were also used for worship and ceremonies, much as churches and synagogues are used today.

What Was Daily Life Like?

The Anasazi gathered on the roof of the pueblo or cliff dwelling. Food was prepared there. Family members wove clothing and made or mended tools. A ladder led to the kiva below.

Artifacts tell us what the Anasazi ate. Grinding tools suggest that they ground foods such as corn, nuts, and seeds. We know that they used painted bowls to serve and store food.

Clay pots were used to cook and serve food.

grinding tools

serving bowl

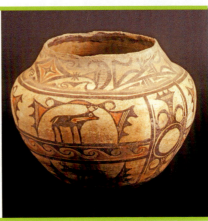

cooking pot

These artifacts tell us more about how the Anasazi lived. What kind of work was done? Was there time for play? What kinds of games were played and by whom? How are the tools found here different from those found in other dig sites? These are just some of the many questions archaeologists ask.

Awls were made of bone. They could be used to poke holes through leather, which allowed the women to sew moccasins together.

game

axes

13

Mesa Verde National Park

In 1906 the area called Mesa Verde became a national park. To date, thousands of artifacts have been found here. The artifacts are labeled and displayed in museums.

Visitors can see artifacts like these in museums.

If you're in Mesa Verde National Park, you can visit Crow Canyon. There, you can work alongside archaeologists and dig for artifacts yourself.

The work of archaeologists gives us a glimpse of the past. Hundreds of years from now, archaeologists may uncover artifacts that tell a story about your town!